30 M
... To Make
Yourself Richer

Niki Chesworth

**KOGAN
PAGE**

YOURS TO HAVE AND TO HOLD

BUT NOT TO COPY

First published in the UK by Kogan Page, 1998

Kogan Page Limited
120 Pentonville Road
London N1 9JN

British Library Cataloguing in Publication Data
A CIP record for this book is available from the British Library.

ISBN 0 7494 2668 3

Typeset by The Florence Group, Stoodleigh, Devon
Printed and bound in Great Britain by Clays Ltd, St Ives plc

CONTENTS

The 30 Minutes Series

The *Kogan Page 30 Minutes Series* has been devised to give your confidence a boost when faced with tackling a new skill or challenge for the first time.

So the next time you're thrown in at the deep end and want to bring your skills up to scratch or pep up your career prospects, turn to the *30 Minutes Series* for help!

Titles available are:

30 Minutes Before Your Job Interview

30 Minutes Before a Meeting

30 Minutes Before a Presentation

30 Minutes to Boost Your Communication Skills

30 Minutes to Brainstorm Great Ideas

30 Minutes to Deal with Difficult People

30 Minutes to Succeed in Business Writing

30 Minutes to Master the Internet

30 Minutes to Make the Right Decision

30 Minutes to Make the Right Impression

30 Minutes to Plan a Project

30 Minutes to Prepare a Job Application

30 Minutes to Write a Business Plan

30 Minutes to Write a Marketing Plan

30 Minutes to Write a Report

30 Minutes to Write Sales Letters

Available from all good booksellers.
For further information on the series, please contact:

Kogan Page, 120 Pentonville Road, London N1 9JN
Tel: 0171 278 0433 Fax: 0171 837 6348

INTRODUCTION

Money. We have many names for it . . . lucre, moolah, dosh, lolly, spondulix, bread, readies, bucks . . . and we have even more uses for it. So many uses in fact, that keeping hold of it, once we have earned it, is not easy.

Although we spend most of our lives working to earn money we put comparatively little effort into making ourselves richer (other than buying lottery tickets or making a quick visit to the bookmakers). You can expect to put in at least 70,000 hours of hard graft during your working life and – even on modest earnings – will be paid around £1 million. Yet when you come to retire the chances are that you will have little of this money left. You will probably look back and wonder where all your earnings went.

The problem with giving advice on money is that most people listen, agree and then – despite their best intentions – ignore it.

It is easy to commit yourself to saving more and spending less, but much harder to do it in practice when there are so many other tempting ways to use your money.

The following might concentrate your mind.

- If you took out the cheapest £50,000 mortgage rather than one with the worst rate, you would pay £8,000 less in interest over the 25-year term of the homeloan.

- Reducing the term of the average 25-year mortgage to just 15 years will cost an extra £100 a month but save more than £33,000 in interest.

- Simply switching a £80,000 mortgage to a 2 percent cheaper fixed or discount rate could save you more than £1,000 in just one year.

- If you had invested £1,000 in the top-performing Personal Equity Plan (PEP) five years ago it would now be worth around £3,000.

- Pick the best-performing endowment and over 25 years your £50 a month investment will pay you £40,000 more than if you select the worst-performing fund.

These savings and gains may not seem to add up to that much and you may be thinking they are hardly going to make you rich. Remember, even if you are only £2,000 or £3,000 better off this year, you would have to have a pay rise of around £4,000 to make this much extra after tax.

If someone stole that amount of money from you, you would probably be tempted to inflict some serious physical damage. By failing to make the most of your money you are robbing yourself.

And how will it make you rich? Wisely invest your £2,000 annual savings by cutting your spending by just £38.50 a week and in ten years you could have £50,000 as a cash lump sum. Double your savings and you will be £100,000 better off.

1

THINK RICH

Many people have a defeatist attitude to finance. 'I'm useless with money', 'I can't understand tax' and 'I haven't got time to sort out my finances' are common exclamations. If you start off with negative thoughts like those you are likely to end up being poorer not richer. The only way you are going to make yourself richer is by thinking positively. Don't be frightened of anything financial – learn everything you can, read the personal finance pages of newspapers and ask questions if you are confused.

The other common problem is that most people don't like to think about money. They hope that if they just struggle along and somehow make ends meet, everything will sort itself out. It won't. You have to make an effort. You have to be proactive rather than reactive. For instance, you feel your bank charges are excessive. Don't delay doing something as the charges will quickly mount up. Complain and if your bank will not refund or review your charges or offer to restructure your borrowing facility to reduce the costs, switch your account to another bank.

Mr Rich	Mr Poor	Mr Rich's saving/gain over 25 years
Paid an extra £100 a month off his £50,000 mortgage so he could pay it off after 15 years	Took out a standard 25-year variable mortgage	£30,000
Bought the best-performing £60 a month endowment	Bought the worst-performing policy	£50,000
Decided to pay in an extra £100 a month to his company pension when he was 30 years old	Thought he did not need to pay any extra contributions because he was in a company scheme	£100,000
Thought one £7-a-week takeaway meal was enough	Liked curry so much he bought two £7 takeaways every week	£9,100
Always remembered to take the video tapes back on time	Paid a £2 fine every week for forgetting to take back his videos	£2,600
Invested the £1,000 bonus given to employees 20 years ago in a top-performing investment trust	Could not believe the company had given him a £1,000 bonus and blew the lot	£28,000
Decided to cut his bills by insulating his home, having an energy efficient boiler, installing thermostats, etc	Thought the savings to be made on energy efficiency were not worth the extra cost	£2,000
Shopped around every year for best motor and household insurance deals	Simply renewed policies every year as he didn't realize he could make large savings	£5,000
Only bought new clothes in the sales – saving 25% every year	Hated all the crowds at the sales so paid the full price	£2,500
Saved £16 a week by not smoking	Smoked five packets of cigarettes a week	£20,800
	Mr Rich's savings/gains	**£250,000**

If your monthly mortgage payments start to soar, don't accept that you have to pay more because interest rates have risen. Switch to a cheaper, fixed-rate or discount mortgage.

Apathy is another common problem. Most people can cut their annual insurance bills – often by as much as £200 – just by switching their policies. However, many automatically renew policies each year without shopping around.

So the golden rules are:

- decide to make yourself richer
- think positively about money
- be pro-active
- always shop around.

Sounds too easy to be true? To demonstrate how simple it is to become richer let's take two hypothetical men aged 50. They live next door to each other, bought their homes at the same time – 25 years ago – and earn exactly the same average salary. For the purposes of this example they are identical in every way except that one – Mr Rich – has been sensible with his money and the other – Mr Poor – has been careless.

As the example on page 8 shows it does not take much effort to be £250,000 better off. And this example only shows the savings for someone on average earnings – the more you earn and save the greater your gains will be. And it excludes the wealth built up in your home, your main pension fund and any investments.

2

MAKE THE MOST OF WHAT YOU'VE GOT

The easiest way to make yourself instantly richer is to make the most of the money you already have.

You could easily boost your spending and investing power by at least 5 or 10 per cent by following the tips in this book.

For example, if you earn £25,000 a year, by prudent money management you could free up £2,000 a year of take-home pay. As a basic rate taxpayer you would have to have a salary increase of £2,600 to give you that much extra spending power. That is equivalent to a 10 per cent pay rise.

Just think how hard you would have to work to get a salary increase that large.

For a fraction of the time and effort involved in boosting your earnings, you can reorganize your finances and make the same financial gains.

Where does your money go?

You will have already wondered about this. You get paid and before you know it all your money has disappeared.

Most of us have a good idea of what we spend our money on, but only by doing a more detailed budget can we work out where savings and gains can be made.

Step one

Flick through your last few months' bank and credit card statements and quickly add up where your money goes. On a piece of paper write out a rough list of expenditure. For instance:

Item of expenditure	Monthly cost/spend
Rent/mortgage	£500
Supermarket	£400
Insurance	£20
Life insurance	£30
Bank credit card charges/interest	£30
Travel costs	£100
Petrol	£40
TV licence/videos/satellite subscription	£30
Takeaways	£40
Lunches at work	£50
Corner shop/incidentals/snacks	£80
Going out	£160
Clothes and shoes (divide approximate annual spend by 12)	£85
Council tax	£60
Newspapers/books/CDs	£50
Dry cleaning, shoe repairs	£25
Savings/investments	£30
TOTAL:	**£1,730**

Remember, this budget does not include items of capital expenditure such as furniture, kitchen equipment, decorating or emergencies such as a new engine for the car.

Step two

Compare your budget with your actual spending. Simply total up how much you actually spent over the last few months and compare it to the total spending figure you have just calculated. The chances are that you spent more than you estimated. For instance:

Total budgeted spend	£1,450
Actual monthly spend	£1,700
Extra spending not accounted for	£250

It is easy to forget where money has gone – it often seems to disappear. Now revise your monthly spending budget.

Step three

Now you have a good idea of where your money goes each month, scrutinize your spending to identify ways to make savings. You should split your outgoings into four categories – necessary, unnecessary, money-down-the-drain and, finally, desirable.

Necessary: your mortgage/rent, household insurance, gas/electricity, telephone, groceries and toiletries, clothes, etc.

Unnecessary: eating out, alcohol, cinema/entertainment, flowers/plants, takeaways, taxis, etc.

Down-the-drain: parking fines, unauthorized overdraft charges, expensive grocery bills at late-night shops, etc.

Desirable: regular savings/investments, pension contributions, etc.

Step four

Work out ways to save money. You will probably already
know if you are spending more than you are earning. Your
overdraft will be getting bigger, you will be owing more and
more on your credit card or you may have had to take out
a loan. Even if you are not spending more than you can
afford, the chances are that you are still spending too much.

Make a commitment right now to stop throwing money
down the drain. We all do it. Sometimes it is unavoidable.
Then decide to cut down on spending your money unnec-
essarily – and stick to your decision. You will be instantly
better off. Some of the following may not apply to you, but
all are good examples of how many people waste money.

- Expensive shopping bills at the corner shop because you
  are too tired to go to the supermarket.

- Taking taxis because you missed the train or bus.

- Bank charges incurred because you exceeded your overdraft limit or did not make time to arrange a facility with
  your bank.

- Paying over-the-odds for things (clothes, cds, furniture,
  etc) because you don't bother to shop around.

Even if you are not wasting money on spending that is not
essential, the chances are that you are still spending too
much on items in your 'necessary' list. These are bills that
you cannot avoid or cut out of your budget, such as gas,
electricity and the telephone. Just because these bills
cannot be avoided doesn't mean they can't be cut. Read
the money-saving tips in the next chapter.

Step five

Now that you have worked out where your money is going
and looked at areas of unnecessary expenditure and ways

to cut your regular bills, it is time to revise your monthly budget. Recalculate your outgoings and try to cut them down as much as possible. But be realistic. Do not commit yourself to spending only £50 a month on going out, if that means you are going to get fed up quickly and give up on your plans to make the most of your money.

Once you have drawn up a revised budget you should stick to it. Review it on a regular basis to find out whether you are exceeding your spending limits or saving more than you expected. As you read this book and learn about other money saving ideas you may want to revise it again. As long as your spending goes down and the amount you save and invest goes up, you will be better off.

3

FREE UP CASH TO START INVESTING

You may think that cutting back on spending is hardly going to make you rich. This is true. But it is the first step. Only when you have freed up spare income and capital can you start to make money.

Are you spending too much?

The chances are that the answer to this question is 'yes'. You can cut the cost of most items of expenditure simply by shopping around. So saving money does not mean you have to go without or are forced to reduce the quality of your lifestyle.

Mortgages

Remortgaging is increasingly popular, with homebuyers changing lenders to slash their monthly repayments. Just because you already have a mortgage does not mean you have to remain with the same lender until you have completely repaid it.

The biggest savings will come from reducing the term of your mortgage – an option that gets little publicity. The drawback is that your monthly repayments will rise as a result. However, you will not only free yourself of the shackles of a mortgage at an earlier age but can also save as much as £60,000 of interest in the process.

Consider switching to a lender that charges interest on a daily basis instead of an annual basis. Most lenders calculate interest basing the next 12 months' payments on the mortgage balance outstanding on the first day of the year. No account is made of payments credited to the repayment mortgage during the year even though the borrower is reducing the amount owed every month. This costs UK borrowers some £160 million a year.

By picking one of the few lenders that calculates interest on a daily basis – on the balance outstanding at the end of each day – the total interest paid is dramatically reduced.

Other alternatives to investigate are:

- switch to a fixed-rate loan
- switch to a discount-rate loan
- add your other loans to your mortgage so you can borrow at a cheaper rate
- increase the term of your mortgage to cut your monthly repayments
- pay lump sums off your mortgage to reduce your monthly bills.

Savings quickly mount up if you restructure your mortgage payments. Here are some examples.

- Someone increasing repayments on a £55,000 mortgage by just 3 per cent a year can save £22,304 in interest and repay their loan eight years early.

- The average homebuyer with a £50,000 mortgage could save almost £16,000 in interest by taking out a 20-year mortgage instead of the usual 25-year homeloan.

- Paying in an additional lump sum of £1,000 a year – from say an annual bonus – every Christmas starting in the second year of a 25-year £50,000 mortgage will not only enable the buyer to repay the loan nine years and five months early but will also save £33,032 in interest, according to Yorkshire Bank. If that £1,000 a year had been put in a building society, it would have to produce net returns of over 10 per cent after tax – or almost 17 per cent gross for a higher rate taxpayer – to make the homebuyer better off investing the cash rather than using it to reduce the mortgage.

- Giving up a £3.25 packet of cigarettes a day and using this cash to reduce a £50,000 mortgage would save £32,225 in mortgage interest payments and reduce the time spent paying the loan by ten years and four months according to Mortgage Trust.

However, if you are considering remortgaging watch out for redemption penalties (these are charges levied if you do not keep your new mortgage going, want to switch to another lender or miss any payments during the first three to five years), arrangement fees and compulsory insurance.

TIP: If you pay off part of your homeloan, check when these additional payments will be credited to your mort-gage. Some lenders require minimum payments of £1,000 and do not credit smaller repayments until the end of the year. In other cases – particularly with fixed-rate or discount loans – you may incur a penalty for paying off part of your loan.

> **TIP:** If you are taking out a mortgage with a new lender pick one that does not charge mortgage indemnity insurance – the insurance homebuyers must take out to protect the lender should the mortgage fall into arrears. Some lenders charge £1,000 or more for this insurance while others make no charge at all.

Insurance

More than six in ten householders are paying well over the odds for their insurance, according to a survey by leading insurance brokers John Charcol. In many cases householders are paying as much as 25 per cent more than they need to and can save up to £200 a year.

If you took out your insurance policy at the same time as your mortgage – shop around. If your lender tries to charge you a £25 fee, move to a 'direct' telephone-based insurer that offers to refund the fee.

The price of house contents insurance is influenced by where you live – right down to your postcode. The risk of burglary is the main factor that pushes up the cost of premiums. By cutting these risks you can make savings.

Household insurance: Ten ways to cut costs

Action	Saving
Shop around	up to 25%
Fit good quality locks	5–15%
Install an approved burglar alarm	up to 15%
Join a neighbourhood watch scheme	up to 5%
Ask for discounts for the over 50s	up to 20%
Find out if there are no claims discounts	5–30%

> **TIP**: Don't skimp by reducing cover. If you under-insure your property or its contents your insurance company will reduce the amount of money it pays out if you make a claim – or it could even reject your claim.

Bank account

If you can make your current account work for you rather than you working to service your bank and interest charges you will not only be richer but will also find managing your money less stressful.

You could easily be spending several hundred pounds a year in unnecessary bank and interest charges if you regularly exceed your overdraft limits. Even if you don't have an overdraft, choosing the right bank account can still save – or make – you money.

Here are the golden rules of banking.

- Avoid bank charges whenever possible. Although banks stopped charging those in credit in 1986 some have started to reintroduce fees for packaged accounts that offer a range of services. So even if you are in credit you could still pay bank charges.

- Be aware that banks and building societies regularly change the terms and conditions of their accounts. These changes may be promoted as a good thing for customers by emphasizing, for instance, that a free overdraft buffer zone of £50 or £100 has been introduced. But read the small print as you may find that charges and overdraft rates have soared.

- Earn interest if you keep your account in credit. But never keep large sums in your current account as you can get better rates of interest in other types of account.

- Never borrow without the consent of your bank because the charges are usually excessive. It will be cheaper to borrow on your credit card than to pay unauthorized overdraft fees.

- Always check your bank statements to ensure that they are correct. A recent survey found that one in three customers spot an error every year.

- Keep a copy of your bank or building society's latest tariff of charges so that you are fully aware of the financial consequences of being overdrawn or using any banking facilities.

- If you are unhappy with the service or charges of your bank or building society – complain. You may get a refund.

- Monitor your bank balance on a regular basis to ensure that you are not overspending or in danger of exceeding your borrowing limits.

You may have a current account that has competitive charges and meets your needs. But the chances are that you could be better off either switching your account or your bank.

The Consumers' Association recently calculated that a borrower with a £500 unauthorized overdraft for one week each quarter would pay £300 per year with one bank but just £65 with another.

TIP: Compare when charges are levied. If you dip into the red once a quarter and are charged on a quarterly basis you will have to pay the maximum bank charges for the entire year. But if you opt for an account with monthly charges you will only have to pay the fee four times a year.

> **TIP**: Also check when charging periods start and finish. You could find that this is just before you are paid so you will be overdrawn at the end of one charging period and the beginning of the next and as such will pay two lots of overdraft fees instead of one.

> **TIP**: Unauthorized overdrafts over a short period of time can have an equivalent annual percentage rate of more than 2,000 per cent. So borrowing on a credit card will be far, far cheaper.

Even on authorized (agreed) overdrafts the difference in cost is vast. The annual cost of going overdrawn by £500 for one week each quarter varies from £3.50 with one building society to £150.35 with one bank.

Credit cards

Always take advantage of any interest-free periods (usually up to 26 or 31 days) but remember you must pay your balance in full to escape interest.

Switch your card to an issuer that does not charge an annual fee unless you regularly have a high outstanding balance, in which case opt for one with a fee and low interest charges.

If your card issuer ups its charges, shop around. Many card issuers waive annual fees in the first year you have the card so once that period is up move on and find another free offer.

If you owe £1,000 at the start of the year, spend £120 a month and repay £140 a month but never pay your balance off entirely, your credit card can cost you under £130 a year

---

TIP: Do not make ATM (cash point) withdrawals using a credit card as you will be charged up to £2 every time you do so. So withdrawing £10 could cost you £2.

---

or more than £220 a year depending on the card issuer, according to *Which?*

If you tend to use your credit card at only two or three shops and pay off your outstanding balance in full each month a storecard could prove more cost effective than a credit card. Although the rate of interest charged on store-cards is usually higher than that charged on credit cards, if you never borrow money on your card the rate will be irrelevant. And storecards do not charge an annual fee.

The advantages are that you can usually get discounts or special shopping benefits as a storecard holder and in some cases storecards may be the only type of credit card accepted in a shop.

Motoring and travel

Running a car is a major expense. In addition to fuel, there is insurance, maintenance and road tax, and do not forget to take into account depreciation, which makes all but some classic cars a bad investment.

Make yourself less of a risk to insurance companies by building up your no-claims discount, taking an advanced driving test, buying a car that is cheaper to insure or parking your vehicle off-the-road or in a garage.

Some insurers charge up to 40 per cent more for the same cover, so always shop around for the best quote.

Don't skimp by taking out reduced cover – for instance only third party instead of fully comprehensive.

Save on fuel costs by thinking twice before getting in your car.

Remember that driving at 70mph can use up to 30 per cent more fuel than driving at 50mph.

Pick a car that suffers less depreciation. If you lose £5,000 off the value of your car in the first few years your net worth will go down not up. Leave buying the car of your dreams until you can really afford it.

Household bills

> **TIP**: If you are sent an estimated bill from a utility company – check your meter reading. If you are not paying enough you could be in for a shock. If you are asked to pay too much, remember you can make better use of your money than allowing a utility to sit on it!

Telephone

Sign up for British Telecom discounts or consider switching to a cable company.

You probably spend between £200 and £300 a year on your telephone bill – if not more. Although it may not seem worthwhile switching phone services to save 50 or so pounds a year, over the long run savings do mount up.

In most cases you will be better off using an alternative to BT. The annual rental of a BT phone is over £100 – almost double the cheapest line rental from a cable company.

> **TIP**: Pay utility bills by direct debit, as that way you cannot forget to pay a bill and you can spread the costs. And you qualify for discounts of up to 14 per cent. However, if your direct debit means you are paying too much ask for it to be cut. You don't want your utility company to owe you money.

The Cable Information Service on 0990 111 777 will tell you if your area has a cable service.

Mobile phone

Choosing the most suitable service provider is essential as if you pick the wrong network, tariff, contract and phone you could be paying far too much for your mobile phone and be tied into a contract that is difficult to get out of.

Your mobile phone (unless you are lucky enough to have one provided by your employer in which case you will still have to pay tax) will cost you around £200 a year.

These are the things to consider.

- ***Tariffs***:   It is important that you choose a tariff that will reflect your needs. Generally, the lower the monthly charge the higher the cost of a call.

- ***When you make calls***:   Just as with land lines, there are different charges for peak and off-peak calls, and some mobile phone providers offer free off-peak local calls at weekends.

- ***Who you will be ringing***:   Some mobile phone service providers charge more for long-distance and national calls than for local calls. Check how the service provider defines a 'local' call.

- ***Whether you will be using it as a messaging service***:   If you intend to receive a high number of messages you can be stung heavily by some service providers. While some may charge 39p to retrieve a message, with other service providers these calls are free.

- ***How calls are charged***:   With digital phones calls are charged by the second but calls made on analogue phones often charge for a minimum of a minute and then in 30-second increments.

- ***Flexibility***:   Can you switch from one tariff to another without financial penalty?

Gas/electricity

Ask your local electricity and gas company for energy-saving tips – most companies produce free guides.

The deregulation of the gas market means that some 19 million consumers can now shop around. You will still have the same gas supplied via the existing pipes and meter. The only difference is who sells you the gas and sends the bill. Watch out for the small print if you plan to switch gas companies. You will have to sign a binding contract and will normally have to pay a fee if you want to cancel the contract early.

Prices will depend on how much gas you use and how you pay, with a discount for those who pay by direct debit. British Gas gives £72 off a £500 annual bill if you pay direct debit. Compare the standing charge as well as the price per unit.

Most householders can save between 10 and 15 per cent on their gas bills by switching suppliers and some as much as 20 per cent. That could be as much as £100 annually.

Here are ten ways to slash your fuel bills.

1. Install low-energy, long-life lightbulbs. They may be more expensive to buy initially, but you can save up to £10 per bulb a year or up to £60 in the bulb's lifetime of up to five years.

2. Draught-proof windows and doors (you can do it yourself) to save up to £20 a year. Lining curtains with a thermal material and keeping them drawn as much as possible will also conserve heat.

3. Lag your hot water tank if it is not already or buy an additional one so the jacket is at least 80mm thick. The savings are up to £10 a year.

4. Make the most of thermostatic radiator valves to regulate the temperature of radiators – the flow of hot water

is reduced once the thermostat reaches a set temperature.

5. If you live in a house rather than a flat, adequate loft insulation of at least 150mm is recommended but remember to lag pipes in the roof space to stop them freezing and to insulate your water tank.

6. Turn down your central heating thermostats by 1 degree – there will be very little difference in temperature – and savings can be up to 10 per cent.

7. Don't leave electrical items switched on or on standby unless you need to. A television can use up to one-third as much power when it's on standby as when it's actually on.

8. If you live in a house built after 1930 and don't already have cavity wall insulation consider it. It can be expensive (£400–£600) but the savings can be up to a quarter of the price each year.

9. If you have your hot water and central heating on timer switches make sure these are used effectively and do not heat up the house or water when you don't need to.

10. If you have a fireplace that you don't use consider blocking it up (don't forget the airbrick for adequate ventilation).

Water

Water metering can save you money – but remember it only pays if you have a high rateable value and low consumption.

Borrowing

Before you borrow money always think about how much you can afford to repay each month – not just how much a lender will offer to lend you – and if you could still meet these payments if interest rates rise. If you cannot meet your repayments your borrowing costs will rise as you may have to pay interest on your outstanding interest, and in the worst scenario you could be taken to court or have your home repossessed.

Many of those who borrow on their credit card or run up an overdraft also have savings and investments. This, does not make financial sense as you would need to earn a fantastic rate of return on your investments to cover the cost of interest and charges.

Borrowing £1,000 on a credit card costs around £200 a year. You would need to earn 20 per cent returns after tax or 34 per cent before tax as a higher rate taxpayer on £1,000 of savings just to break even.

Compare the annual percentage rate (APR) when borrowing money. This shows the true cost of interest over a year and includes interest and one-off charges. The lower the ARP the better the deal. However, it does not include credit insurance which many lenders push customers into buying.

The best borrowing options for you will depend on how long you want to borrow for.

- **Short term**: overdrafts or credit cards may work out cheaper than personal loans. Overdrafts linked to gold charge cards can also be good value but don't forget to take into account the annual fee.

- **Longer term**: (a year or more) personal loans, secured loans.

Often you will find that shops, double glazing companies, kitchen manufacturers, car showrooms and so on offer credit facilities. Unless the credit is interest free or at a preferentially low rate, you should be aware that interest rates may be higher than those of a bank loan.

TIP: Ask whether there are any penalties if you pay off your loan early. For instance you may be charged interest for an extra two months rather than for just the time period you have borrowed the money. So be careful not to take out a loan for longer than you need.

TIP: You may not be given a written quotation but you must be given one if you ask. It is better to read it at home when you have time to study it carefully. Most loan application forms include some form of credit protection insurance but you may have to tick a box if you *don't* want it rather than opting for it.

TIP: You can't cancel a credit deal if you sign it in a trader's shop, office or other business premises. You can only cancel if you signed the form at home. Unless you can see a box entitled 'Your right to cancel' you will not be able to do so. Be wary of agreeing deals over the phone because you cannot cancel a credit agreement arranged on the phone, even if you sign it at home.

If you pay off your loan early, you may find that you have to pay some of the interest you would have had to pay should the loan have run its full term. However, this is often confusingly called a 'rebate' of the interest you would have paid. A rebate may sound like you are benefiting but you are not – the extra interest you must pay is in effect a penalty.

Always read the small print, and read through the terms and conditions before signing.

If you are planning to borrow larger amounts over a longer period consider a secured loan – one that uses your property or another asset such as a life insurance policy as security. Rates tend to be lower than for other types of loan and repayments are lower because the loan is usually over a longer period. Weigh up the pitfalls of securing the loan on your home against the savings in borrowing costs and don't forget to take into account any extra costs such as valuation and legal fees.

You can either approach your mortgage lender for a further advance on your mortgage – which will probably be the cheapest option – or approach a separate lender.

In some cases you can use other assets such as endowment policies as security for a loan (ask your life insurance company for details).

4

GET ORGANIZED

Being organized is vital if you want to make yourself richer. Why? Because if you do not keep track of your finances, you will not be able to avoid unnecessary expenses or make the most of investment opportunities.

Set up a filing system so that you always know where to find all your financial paperwork such as:

- bank statements
- credit card statements
- mortgage details/MIRAS forms/annual statements
- insurance
- warranties and guarantees
- receipts.

How can this save you money?

Next time your dishwasher, television, video or washing machine breaks down, how will you know if it is still covered by a warranty or guarantee if you can't find the paperwork?

When your car or home insurance comes up for renewal, how will you know if your premiums have soared if you have not kept a record of how much you paid last year?

When you are filling in your tax return or talking to your tax adviser how will you know if you are claiming every allowance available and making the most of tax-efficient investments, if you do not know your current financial position?

If you are organized you will also be able to:

- avoid late payment penalties on bills, tax payments, etc

- make the most of discounts for prompt payment/ payment by direct debit

- spot errors on bank or credit card statements

- review the interest rates on your savings accounts to make sure you are still getting the best deal

- check your mortgage is still competitive

- compare renewal costs of insurance policies with what you paid last year

- find the relevant paperwork quickly if you decide to buy or sell an investment to make a profit

- check you are making the most of tax breaks given on pension investments

- make the most of tax rules covering capital gains tax.

So that you can make the most of the moneymaking ideas featured in this book, do not waste time on your day-to-day finances. Set up direct debits to pay bills so you qualify for discounts and avoid financial penalties should you forget to pay them on time. This will also help you budget as the cost of major bills – such as for gas and electricity – can be spread over 12 months.

Using a computer

One of the easier ways to organize your finances, particularly if you are computer literate, is using your personal computer. There are several stand-alone software programs that allow you to organize your accounts at home or draw up your own using a spread sheet.

You can also use the internet to find out information on anything from savings accounts to share prices. Some banks and building societies offer home banking. These allow you to do your banking at a time to suit you – 24 hours a day.

You can combine your monthly budget, financial goals and details of your net worth on a spread sheet. This will help you to alter figures as the amount you invest and the amount you are worth increases.

5

PROTECTING WHAT YOU'VE GOT

Before you get carried away with spending, saving or investing any of this extra cash you will be accumulating, you must first make sure you have protected your assets and your income.

Insuring your assets

You probably already have motor, house and contents insurance in place. But you should also check that you have adequate cover and that you increase this cover as your assets grow in value.

Another type of insurance that is often overlooked is mortgage protection insurance. There is little point in investing in property if you risk losing your home because you cannot keep up your mortgage repayments after you lose your job or cannot work due to ill health.

Protecting your income

There are several types of policy that can provide cover.

- **_Permanent health insurance_**: this is particularly important for the self-employed and provides an income should you become too ill to work.

- **_Critical illness insurance_**: this provides you with a lump sum should you suffer a major, life-threatening or terminal illness such as cancer.

- **_Payment protection/credit insurance_**: if you are borrowing a significant amount of money including a mortgage you will probably be recommended to take out payment protection insurance by the person or company arranging your loan. This covers your payments should you lose your income because of illness or if you are made redundant.

Protecting your family

Life insurance is also important. This will protect the wealth of your family should the worst happen. You should buy adequate insurance to cover your outstanding mortgage and other debts, as well as to provide your family with enough capital – and therefore income.

6

HOW RICH ARE YOU?

Now you have decided to make the most of your income and made sure you have protected what you already own, you should get your assets working for you. But first you need to know how much you are really worth.

Add up the value of everything you own and owe. Here is an example.

	Value	
ASSETS:		
House	£75,000	
Pension fund	£35,000	
Shares	£2,000	
Savings	£1,000	
Endowment (on maturity)	£90,000	
Chattels (furniture, etc)	£11,000	
TOTAL:		£214,000

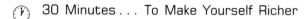

BORROWINGS:		
Mortgage	£60,000	
Credit card	£800	
Personal loan	£2,000	
TOTAL:		− £62,800
NET WORTH:		= £151,200

This is your balance sheet. Every time you buy a new asset or it increases in value revise the figures. And when you reduce your borrowings do the same.

As the money-making tips in this book start to pay dividends so your net worth will increase. Updating these figures on a regular basis will not only help you to monitor how successful you are at making money but a quick look at your balance sheet will also make you feel richer. You will find this a powerful motivator to making even more money in the future.

7

HOW RICH DO YOU WANT TO BE?

Now that you know where you stand financially and have worked out how much money comes in and out, you can look at your motivation for wanting to make more money.

You would not be reading this book if you did not want to be richer. But you need to know why. If you have ever read an interview with a successful and wealthy person you will know that very few say that their aim in life is to be rich. They either make their money because they want to be the best at their chosen career or because they are driven to succeed by a desire for a particular lifestyle. Only if you have a clear idea of what you want to achieve, will you be able to achieve it.

As an incentive to keep within your budget and to help you achieve your ideal financial situation you should set yourself targets. These may be cutting your overdraft, saving up for a deposit on a new house or buying a new car.

You should set short-term goals as well as longer term ones so that you are rewarded more quickly for the efforts you have just made. The following are examples of the things you may want to include on your list of goals.

Short-term goals:

● Cut monthly spending by £100

● Reduce overdraft by £200 a month

● Save £50 a month

● Switch borrowings to cheaper rates

● Start a pension.

Medium-term goals:

● Pay off overdraft/eliminate borrowing completely

● Save up for a new home/car/round-the-world trip

● Build up an investment portfolio.

Longer-term goals:

● Invest enough to retire at 50

● Become financially secure

● Build up a lump sum to start your own business.

Once you have decided on your goals put timescales against each one and stick your list where you can see it every day. It will help to motivate you.

As you achieve each goal update your list and set yourself new targets. But remember this will only work if you really want to achieve each goal. There is no point in writing down 'Invest to build up £50,000 in five years' time' if you don't make every effort to achieve that goal. So be realistic otherwise you will feel disappointed and may be tempted to give up.

8

SPECULATE TO ACCUMULATE

Now that your day-to-day finances are in order, and you know how to control and reduce your spending and cut your borrowing costs, you should have freed up some income to start making serious money.

Remember it is important to get the basics right first. That way you do not need to waste time tracking down bills or payments and do not need to waste money on things like excessive bank charges or over-the-top insurance premiums.

So what should you do with your cash?

Safety-net savings

Always keep a stash of cash for use in emergencies and so you can take advantage of investment opportunities. But never consider savings as a long-term investment as your money is likely to go down in real terms.

Although savings rates are currently above inflation this has not always been the case, with savers being left with less spending power even after interest than when they first invested their cash.

Ideally, your stash of cash should cover three months' bills.

Tax-free investments

Make the most of every tax break you can get but only if the underlying performance is good. Remember, you will be better off making 6 per cent returns after tax than 3.5 per cent returns tax free.

At the time of writing this book the most popular tax-free investments, the Personal Equity Plan or PEP and the Tax Exempt Special Savings Account or TESSA, were due to be replaced by the Individual Savings Account (ISA).

Make the most of the tax breaks offered to those investing in PEPs and TESSAs if you can invest before April 1999, and afterwards invest the maximum in savings accounts or shares through the ISA to ensure they grow free of tax.

The other major tax breaks are offered by venture capital trusts and Enterprise Investment Schemes which give tax relief at 20 per cent when you invest up to £100,000, provided you hold your investment for at least five years. They invest in growing, unquoted companies so there is an element of risk. However, the 20 per cent tax relief is not to be sniffed at. Once you have got your basic investments sorted out, look at these schemes as an addition to your investment portfolio.

Pensions also offer generous tax breaks. However, you cannot get your hands on this cash until you retire so they are not for those looking for short-term gains.

Tax relief comes in two forms.

- Tax relief at your top rate of tax when you pay in contributions. So higher rate taxpayers only have to contribute £60 for £100 to be paid into their pension fund – the extra £40 is tax relief.

- The fund grows free of tax. So any investment growth is not taxed, giving higher growth than most other types of investments.

You can invest 15 per cent of your earnings in a company pension scheme, receive a pension of two-thirds of your final salary and take up to one-and-a-half times your final salary as a tax-free lump sum.

If you are not in a company pension scheme, take out a personal pension. You can invest 17.5 per cent of your earnings rising with age to 40 per cent and can take a quarter of your pension fund on retirement (or from the age of 50 if you choose) as a tax-free lump sum.

> **TIP**: Make the most of the tax relief on pensions – it is very generous. Either top up your contributions to your company pension scheme using an Additional Voluntary Contribution scheme or pay in extra monthly contributions to your personal pension.

> **TIP**: Start paying into your pension as soon as possible. If your fund grows at 9 per cent a year and you pay in £100 a month, your pension fund at retirement will be worth £365,000 if you start your plan at the age of 25. By waiting until you are 40 the fund's value will drop to £98,100 and by delaying until you are 50 it will be worth just £35,700.

Playing the stockmarket

Over the longer term the stockmarket is the best place to invest your cash as returns not only beat inflation (unlike most savings accounts), but also produce substantial growth.

If you had deposited £100 in a bank or building society in 1945, today it would be worth £1,000. The same amount invested in the stockmarket could be worth £30,000, if you had reinvested your dividends.

Don't be afraid of the stockmarket. You can start to invest with as little as £20 a month and still have your money invested by a professional fund manager.

The booming stockmarket in recent years has accounted for much of the increase in individual wealth.

Table 8.1: Personal sector net wealth (£ billion)

1986	£1,400
1989	£2,248
1992	£2,376
1995	£2,831
1997	£3,270

Table 8.1 shows that every man, woman and child in the UK is worth over £60,000.

Despite the fact that more than two-thirds of us own our homes, share-based investments – not property – account for much of this wealth.

As Table 8.2 shows, financial assets now account for more of our wealth than tangible assets such as property. This is partly due to the recent property price slump which started in 1989 – prices did not rise back to their pre-price boom levels until early 1998 in many parts of the UK. But

Table 8.2: Where our wealth comes from

	Tangible wealth	Financial assets
1987	56%	44%
1997	41%	59%

Source: Office of National Statistics

Table 8.3: Increasing number of shareholders

Year	No. of individuals owning shares directly
1963	5m
1979	3m
1990	11m
1996	9.5m
1998	15m

Source: ProShare

it is also due to the fact that more of us now own shares – directly and indirectly.

The shift in wealth is also down to how well investments have performed. Over the two years to March 1998 share prices rose by more than 50 per cent, while house prices increased by only 12 per cent.

Timing is everything

At the time of writing this book the stockmarket was at an all-time high – not normally a good time to invest. However, many bears (those who have a negative view on the stock-market) were saying the market was heading for a crash two years earlier – but the market still kept growing. The bulls (those who feel the market will keep rising) may be yet proved right.

But predicting the exact timing of a market fall is a bit like predicting the winning lottery numbers. Even the experts do not always get it right. So as an individual investor you should adopt a different approach.

To reduce the risks of investing at the wrong time – for example just before the market crashes as it did in 1987 – take a long-term view as any rises and falls will be evened out over the long run. And don't panic. Most of those who invested at the beginning of 1987 were still better off by the end of the year. But those who bought at the top of the market and then sold when it fell lost substantially.

Alternatively, try what is known as 'pound-cost-averaging'. Drip feed money into the market on a monthly basis. When the stockmarket falls you will buy more shares for your money and when it rises you buy less. This averages out the price you pay for shares and eliminates the risk of buying at the wrong time. However, those who invest a lump sum at the right time will still make the bigger profit.

The long-term view versus short-term gains

As explained above share-based investments are not for short-termists. Why? The answer is the cost of investing.

Charges usually take a minimum of 5 per cent of the investment if you are buying unit trusts or pooled investments. If you are buying shares the costs will be roughly £15 to £20 minimum or 0.75–1 per cent of the total purchase cost plus 0.5 per cent stamp duty.

In addition, with all stockmarket-based investments there is a bid/offer spread – the difference between the buying price and selling price, which can be as much as 5 per cent. This is similar to the spread when you buy foreign currency. So even if you buy and sell a share at the same price you will still lose out. Only once your investments have increased to cover these costs and inflation will you be as well off as when you first bought your shares or investment funds.

Give your money time to grow

The effects of compounding – earning money on money you have earned as well as on your initial investment – significantly increase your chances of making some serious sums. Even if you had only picked an average performing PEP five years ago, a £5,000 investment would have almost doubled in value.

At an annual growth rate of 9 per cent, money doubles after 8 years and quintuples within 19 years.

Watch out for inflation

The days of rampant inflation may seem like a long time ago when inflation is around 2.5–3 per cent. However, the effects of inflation should still be taken into account. The only way to achieve capital appreciation is by getting 'real' returns after the effects of inflation have been deducted.

To go back to the example given earlier in this chapter, the £100 invested in 1945 would – in real terms – be worth just £50 if you had put it in a building society. The real return on the stockmarket investment, however, would be worth £1,400.

Investment options

People invest in the stockmarket in different ways. Although you may not consider yourself to be playing the market you probably own shares indirectly – through your company or personal pension fund and/or through your endowment policy.

Direct investments in shares include buying individual shares and pooled investments such as unit trusts, PEPs and investment bonds.

Individual shares

This is usually one of the most expensive ways to play the stockmarket and among the most risky. Unless you have a large investment portfolio and pay a stockbroker a hefty fee to advise you on which shares to buy, the dealing costs of buying shares can mean you need substantial growth in order to just break even.

For example, if you bought £1,000 of shares you would probably pay at least £20 in dealing costs and a further £5 in stamp duty. So 2.5 per cent of your investment has gone already. Then you must take into account the 'bid to offer' spread – the difference between the buying price and selling price of shares. It means that if you buy £1,000 of shares and sell them for exactly the same price you may only get £950 back. The difference between the two prices applies to many financial transactions from buying and selling shares to foreign currency (you may have noticed that when you go on holiday you get a different rate for your francs and pesetas if you are buying or selling). And you should also take inflation into account. If your shares grow 2.5 per cent in a year this may not even be enough to keep pace with the cost of living.

So even before you start investing you will need to make at least 5 to 10 per cent returns just to break even.

However, this does not mean that shares are a bad buy – just that you should understand the risks and the fact that you may have to invest for the long term in order to make substantial gains.

How the stockmarket works

The stockmarket has several different share indices. The one you may have heard about is the FTSE 100 – known as the footsie. This is the Financial Times Stock Exchange Index of the top 100 companies in the UK. These shares are also known as 'blue chip'. You are unlikely to lose money because of the company going bust and as such these shares are usually much safer bets.

Other indices are the All-Share index, which does not actually contain all UK companies, only some 900; the FTSE 250 – the top 250 companies; the FTSE 350; and smaller companies. The Alternative Investment Market (the AIM) is the junior stockmarket where smaller and newer companies are first quoted before moving up to the main stockmarket. Generally, the smaller the company and the newer it is to the stockmarket the more risky investing in it will be.

Risk versus reward

With most investments there is a risk versus reward ratio – which dictates that the higher the risk the higher potential rewards. Penny shares – which, as their name implies – have a share value of just a few pence are a prime example of this. If the share rises from 2p to 4p you will double your money. But if the share value drops from 2p to 1p your investment will be halved.

How you make money from shares

As a shareholder you can make money in one of two ways:

- the value of the shares increase as the fortunes and profits of the company increase, and usually in line with general rises in the stockmarket and improvements in the economy as a whole

- the company pays its shareholders a dividend – a share of the profits of the company. This payment can also take the form of extra shares. Not all of the company's profits are used to pay dividends – and if the company suffers a loss dividends may be paid even though there are no profits.

However, remember that shares can go down as well as up and should the company fail you may get little – if any – of your original investment back.

Reading the financial pages

The first thing to know is that the price of shares quoted in the financial pages is not the actual price you will pay if you are buying shares or the price you will receive if you sell them. It is the mid price – the difference between the two.

The financial pages will usually tell you recent price movements, and the highest and lowest price of the share over the last year.

The earnings per share (EPS) tells you the after-tax profit divided by the number of shares in the company.

The price/earnings (p/e) ratio is also key. This is the price or value per share divided by the EPS. Companies can be worth anything between 5 and 25 times their earnings. Generally a high p/e ratio means the shares are in high demand because future profits look good.

Shares you should take up

If you are offered shares in a building society or life insurance company flotation – known as a demutualization – you usually get these free and they are often priced so that there will be instant gains. As such they are worth adding to your portfolio. No wonder they are known as 'windfall' shares. These share offerings are similar to privatizations in that they are often a one-way bet.

If you had invested £1,000 in each of the UK privatization issues and held on to them, you would have invested a total of £22,000 which would now be worth around £200,000.

Share options which are usually offered to employees through a Save-As-You-Earn (SAYE) savings scheme are another good bet. You can invest up to £250 a month in a savings scheme which grows free of tax to buy shares after five years. The advantage is that the price you pay for the shares is the price agreed when you first started saving (five years earlier), so if the company you work for has done well you should be able to buy shares very cheaply. If the shares have done badly there is no risk – you can simply take the cash you have saved (plus interest) instead of buying the shares.

Picking a share

There are several ways to pick the shares you want to invest in.

- Go to a stockbroker and ask for advice. However you may find that this is expensive and only worthwhile if you have a share portfolio of £10,000 or more. For a discretionary service – where the stockbroker manages and invests your share portfolio – the minimum investment is usually £50,000.

- Go to a stockbroker or investment manger who provides investment advice on a group basis – usually through a newsletter. This is cheaper as you are not receiving individual investment advice but are simply taking advantage of share tips given to all the broker's clients.

- Make your own decisions by reading the financial columns of newspapers and reading individual companies' annual reports and accounts.

- Join or form an investment club. These are groups of private investors who join together to pool information and research on which shares to buy. There are about 1,700 investment clubs in Britain. In the US the legendary Beardstown Ladies from a small town near Chicago have managed to produce returns of 24 per cent over the last decade – a return double that of the American market at large.

For more information on buying shares and forming or joining an investment club contact ProShare on 0171 394 5200.

It also helps to understand why shares rise and fall. If a merger or take-over is on the cards shares often soar. Pick a growing new-technology or biotech company that invents the latest software or a new cancer drug and you will reap the rewards. However, if the sector the share is in is expected to suffer – for example, retailers will usually see a fall-off in sales following an interest rate hike – most of the shares in that sector will be marked down as a result.

Golden rules

- Don't panic – if shares tumble, hold tight as they are bound to recover. Never sell at the bottom of a market.

- If you make a mistake and pick a dud, cut your losses and get out quick. As with all aspects of life you win some and you lose some.

- Take a long-term view – three to five years at least.

- Read the financial pages of newspapers to monitor your investment and to be aware of any problems such as a profits warning.

Finding a stockbroker

First of all, ask friends or relatives if they have used a financial adviser or stockbroker that they trust.

If you want to take sharebuying seriously contact the Assocation of Private Client Investment Managers and Stockbrokers (APCIMS) on 0171 247 7080 for a list of members. It may be worth paying a bit extra for an advisory service – not as expensive as a discretionary service where the stockbroker manages your portfolio for you – but which will still give you pointers as to what shares to consider.

If you do not want any advice opt for one of the cheap 'execution only' dealers which simply execute your share deals for as little as £10 or £15 a trade.

Once you become more experienced set up an account with a stockbroker so when you get a good tip or spot a good bargain you can deal over the telephone.

Pooled investments

As described above, there are inherent risks in buying individual shares. For a start if you buy and sell regularly the costs can erode any gains. Second, you are relying on just a few shares to perform well. Third, investment advice can be expensive.

Pooled investments overcome these drawbacks by combining the cash of hundreds – if not thousands – of investors into one big fund. This is then used to buy a wide range of shares and other investments which are professionally managed on your behalf.

There are several different types of pooled investment.

- **Unit trusts**:   Charges are usually 5 per cent of your initial investment plus an annual management fee of 1.5 per cent. Performance does vary so it is essential to pick the right trust. Investors buy units – or shares – in the fund and the value of these units rises and falls depending on the underlying value of the whole investment fund.

- **Investment trusts**:   These are not funds as such. Investors buy a share in an investment trust company quoted on the stock exchange. In turn, the investment trust company invests in other shares and investments such as property or bonds. Buying shares in investment trusts is similar to buying shares in any company. However, there are some major differences. Investment

51

trust shares can trade at a discount – which means the total value of all the shares is less than the value of all the investments owned by the investment trust. So if this discount narrows investors stand to make even more profits. If it widens – they lose. The other major difference is that it is possible to buy shares in investment trusts very cheaply through regular savings schemes.

- **Open-ended investment companies**: These are known as oeics and are similar to unit trusts but they are listed on the stockmarket.

- **PEPs/ISAs**: These are tax-free 'wrappings' round other investments like unit trusts, shares and investment trusts. Until April 1999 you can invest up to £9,000 tax free each year in a PEP. These schemes will then be replaced by the new ISA with a maximum investment of £5,000 a year. Self-select PEPs enable you to invest in individual shares – usually for a minimum dealing charge of £15 per share and an annual management charge of £25 to £250 depending on the amount invested.

- **Single premium bonds**: These are offered by life insurance companies and include an element of life insurance cover. Special tax concessions make them better value for higher rate taxpayers.

- **Broker bonds**: These are investment funds managed by an investment adviser.

- **Friendly society policies**: These are worth considering despite high charges because they are tax free. However, you can only invest up to £270 a year.

Picking the right fund
Most funds actually fail to match the performance of the stockmarket as a whole – even though they are

professionally managed. This has led to the introduction of what are known as unit trust tracker funds, which – as their name implies – aim to track a stockmarket index, either the FTSE or the All-Share. Charges tend to be lower than for other funds as these funds are not actively managed. While these funds will not outperform the stockmarket they should at least manage to do as well as the market. However, pick the right actively managed fund rather than a tracker fund and you will see bigger gains.

So, in 1997 for example, the All-Share index rose by 23 per cent but the top-performing funds produced growth of 38 per cent. However, not all investors were so lucky. Those investing £100 at the start of the year could have seen their initial investment fall to just £70 or less by picking a poor performing fund – such as one investing in the Far East.

There are several things to take into account when picking a fund:

- **Past performance**: But opt for consistently good returns rather than a fund that is a top performer one year and a poor performer the next.

- **Sectors**: Most funds are split into sectors such as UK Equity Growth, European, North American, Far Eastern, High Income and UK Smaller Companies. Although picking the right sector is important, remember that individual funds within each sector perform differently.

- **The fund manager**: A fund manager with a good track record of picking a good stock or unearthing share bargains is important.

- **Charges**: High charges can eat into investment returns. But remember you may be better off picking a high charging fund that produces high returns than a low charging fund with poor returns.

WARNING: Avoid high-risk investments as these are normally complex and should be left up to the experts. These include warrants, futures and options and penny shares. Also avoid any scheme that promises you will 'get rich quick'. If it was that simple the experts would be following this advice. Generally, these schemes are high risk and you could 'get poor quick' instead.

Indirect stockmarket investments

Although the number of private investors in the stockmarket has soared in recent years, the amount held in individual shares is only a fraction of the money most have tied up in the stockmarket.

Pensions and life insurance are the indirect forms of stockmarket investments that can really make you wealthy. Some £1,300 billion of personal assets is held in these types of investments, with about three-quarters of life and pension fund money invested in shares.

Endowments

Although less popular than in the 1980s, in the UK we invest in some 60 million endowment policies, most of them linked to mortgages. They tend to produce lower returns than the best unit trust funds, are inflexible and have higher charges than other stockmarket-based investments.

However, returns are still good for comparatively little monthly outlay. If you had invested £50 a month for 25 years in a top-performing with-profits policy you would have received a cash lump sum of £121,000 on maturity. The average return was £102,000 and the worst £84,000 – still a handsome return compared to under £36,000 in a building society account, but still far below the £173,000 you would have received from the average UK general equity unit trust and £281,000 from the top-performing UK equity fund. But you must remember that for your money you have also received life insurance cover – something you would probably have to pay for even if you did not have an endowment policy.

Golden rules

Never cash in an endowment policy before its term is up – you will suffer. To get the maximum returns policies must be held for the full term. If you are strapped for cash, find out if you can borrow against your endowment. As a last resort try to sell your policy rather than surrendering it – you could receive 15 per cent more.

Pensions

You may feel a pension is not the ideal investment as you cannot take your money until you retire – or until the age of 50 if you invest in a personal pension.

However, very generous tax breaks and the long-term effects of compounding can make pensions one of the best investments you will ever make – particularly if your employer is also paying into your pension fund.

Bonds

Although these are not shares, they are another way to play the stockmarket. Bonds usually pay out a fixed amount each year and come in several forms.

- ***Gilts***: Issued by the British government and also known as gilt-edged securities because they carry no risk of default.

- ***Overseas government bonds***: Usually issued by third world countries and often very risky.

- ***Preference shares***: A mixture of shares and bonds – they are shares that pay a fixed regular dividend.

- **_Convertibles_**:   These give you the option to buy shares at a set price at a later date.

- **_Permanent-income bearing shares_**:   These are issued by building societies to raise cash.

There are several problems with bonds. First, while the income may be fixed the underlying value of your investment is not and you can find that you sell your bond for far less than you bought it for. Second, if you want to make yourself wealthy investing for income is not a good idea – you want long-term growth. And third, in recent years low interest rates mean that bond yields have have not been good – hence the popularity of shares.

9

GETTING ADVICE

Getting financial advice is easy – some 75,000 individuals are authorized to give investment advice. It's getting the right advice that is hard. Before taking out a mortgage or a pension, or investing, you should at least ask a professional for advice.

It is best to go to an independent financial adviser who can survey a range of products available before recommending the most suitable to meet your needs, rather than one who is tied or employed by a life insurance company. Although this advice may appear to be free, the adviser does earn commission for selling you a product. Find out how much this is. Some fee-based financial advisers rebate the commission they would have earned in exchange for a fee. Although you may be reluctant to pay for advice when you can get it free, the commission rebated can often far exceed the fee you pay, making this worthwhile. You have the added protection that the financial adviser is not simply recommending the product that pays the adviser the highest commission.

IFA Promotion on 0117 971 1177 will supply a list of independent financial advisers in your area. The register of fee-based advisers is run by Money Management – call 0117 976 9444.

Golden rules:

- go to at least three financial advisers
- check the adviser is authorized under the Financial Services Act (call 0171 929 3652).
- check the adviser's qualifications and ask how long they have been giving advice
- if you are buying a particular product like a pension opt for an adviser that specializes in this area
- if you are confused by any of the jargon ask for an explanation. If you are still confused the adviser obviously does not understand the product well enough to explain it to you in simple terms.

10

INVESTING IN PROPERTY

Despite the property price slump of the late 1980s and early 1990s, over the longterm bricks and mortar have proved a sound investment.

But there is an inherent difficulty in viewing property as an investment. Most of us are emotionally attached to our homes and therefore do not view them as dispassionately as we would if we were a property developer.

To treat property as an investment we would have to live in an up-and-coming area where prices are likely to rise, even if we would not choose to live there. When it comes to improving the property – something as a nation we spend £30 billion a year doing – we would have to spend on the improvements most likely to make money, not those that would enhance our enjoyment of our homes. And we would have to buy and sell at the right time – when the market dictates, not when our lives dictate.

So, for most of us, it is a question of striking a balance between making money out of our homes while still living where we want to and how we want to.

We all know people who got on to the property ladder in the right place at the right time and as a result are far wealthier than us. One way to make money is to borrow as much as you can – as the more expensive the property the more chance for gains. A 10 per cent price increase on a £50,000 property is only £5,000. On a £150,000 property it is £15,000. However, do not borrow more than you can afford and take out insurance to pay your monthly repayments should you lose your job.

The main advantage of buying is that over the longer term your monthly repayments go down in real terms. The sum of £75,000 borrowed today may seem large but in ten years' time wage, price and property price inflation will mean that in 'real terms' this debt is far lower. Renters, on the other hand, will usually see their rents increase with inflation.

To put this into context, the Abbey National recently calculated that buying a four-bedroom family house in Greater London will save a buyer £200,000 over the life of a 25-year mortgage compared to someone renting the same property. The average saving from buying rather than renting is nearly £100,000 over 25 years.

Just as shares have proved a good investment over the long term, but only if you picked the right ones, the same applies to property – you have to pick the right property in the right area.

Although house price inflation may seem high over the longer term, as a general rule it only rises in line with wage increases. However, between 1985 and 1997 it grew by less than average earnings.

So always view any house price increases in the context of real growth – after inflation – and remember that even if you sell at a profit, you will generally have to buy another property so you are unlikely to come out with any cash in your hand. Only when you reach the empty-nest stage of life when your children have left home, can you start to move down the property ladder and cash in on your gains.

Having said this, an expensive and good quality home does make you feel richer. So even if it does not make you wealthy you will feel wealthier as a result.

Table 10.1: How house prices have risen

Year	Average house price
1957*	£2,330
1967	£4,080
1977	£13,712
1987	£42,546
1997	£75,374

*New homes only
Source: Council of Mortgage Lenders

Buying to rent

Another way to make money out of the property market is to buy homes to rent. Not only do you get capital appreciation but an income as well – which should cover your borrowing costs. The popularity of this option has led to new types of mortgage for would-be private landlords.

Although you should be able to cover your costs, remember rents are not guaranteed. You could lose out if it becomes difficult to find a tenant for several months or – worse – if your tenants fail to pay the rent.

11

ALTERNATIVE INVESTMENTS

Everything from racehorses and fine wines to antiques and classic cars can be considered an investment.

Although there are several companies offering schemes to private investors wanting to cash in on reported price rises of these alternative investments, be careful. As investors have learned in the past everything from whisky to ostrich farming can be risky. So do not start to consider these schemes until you have enough money to afford to lose some of it.

Always avoid 'get-rich-quick' schemes – they usually only make the person selling them rich.

SUMMARY:
Welcome to
a wealthy future

Now that you have read this book you should not only feel more confident about making yourself richer, but also have a good idea of how you are going to achieve this.

Although 30 minutes is not long enough to make yourself seriously wealthy and it may take you as long as 30 years, by putting in place today what you have learned you should ensure that money is never a worry for you again.